CATERHAM AND TATTENHAM CORNER

Vic Mitchell and Keith Smith

MP Middleton Press

First published January 1994

ISBN 1 873793 251

© *Middleton Press 1993*

Design - Deborah Goodridge
Typesetting - Barbara Mitchell
               Deborah Goodridge

Published by Middleton Press
               Easebourne Lane
               Midhurst
               West Sussex
               GU29 9AZ
               Tel: (0730) 813169
(From 16 April 1995 - (01730) 813169)

Printed & bound by Biddles Ltd,
               Guildford and Kings Lynn

CONTENTS

1. Purley area   1- 17
2. Caterham branch   18- 53
3. Tattenham Corner branch   54-120

INDEX

42	Caterham
70	Chipstead
18	Kenley
80	Kingswood
1	Purley
16	Purley Shed
56	Reedham
60	Smitham
90	Tadworth
100	Tattenham Corner
28	Whyteleafe
37	Whyteleafe South
66	Woodmansterne

ACKNOWLEDGEMENTS

We are immensely grateful to those mentioned in the photographic credits for the assistance received and also to R.M.Casserley, D.Clayton, J.H.Clifford, Dr. E.Course, G.Croughton, C.Hall, J.R.W.Kirkby, N.Langridge, A.Ll.Lambert, A.C.Mott, Mr D. & Dr S.Salter, N.Stanyon, E.Wilmshurst, T.Wright and our ever helpful wives.

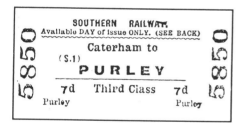

Railway Magazine 1957

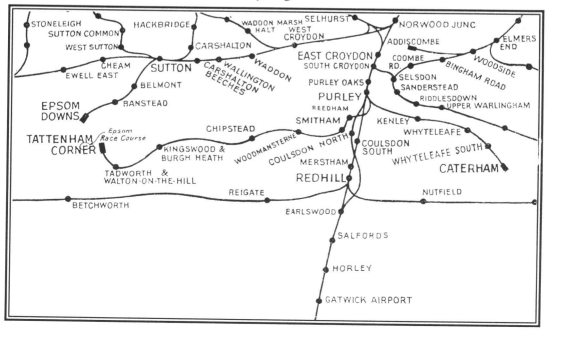

GEOGRAPHICAL SETTING

Both branches are situated in valleys on the dip slope of the chalk of the North Downs. There are no water courses of note, these being technically "dry valleys" on porous chalk.

From 220ft above sea level at Purley the Caterham branch rises to 430ft at its terminus, while its companion passes through the Chipstead Valley to climb to 490ft at Tattenham Corner. The two tunnels on this route were built to protect the environment and not for engineering reasons.

All maps in this album are to the scale of 25" to 1 mile.

HISTORICAL BACKGROUND

Caterham branch

The first line in the area was the horse-worked 1805 Croydon, Merstham and Godstone Railway which never reached Godstone, but did connect with the Surrey Iron Railway to Wandsworth at Croydon.

The London & Brighton Railway was opened between Croydon and Haywards Heath on 12th July 1841, becoming part of the London, Brighton and South Coast Railway in 1846.

The South Eastern Railway's attempt to build a more direct line from London to Dover via Oxted was thwarted by politicians who thought (as again now) they knew best how to operate railways. They forced the LBSCR to share their line between Croydon and Reigate Junction (now Redhill) with the SER. This resulted in the LBSCR owning the line south to Stoats Nest (near Coulsdon) and the SER the other half of the section. An agreement was made between the two companies that they would regard this main line as a boundary between their exclusive territories.

An independent Caterham Railway Company received its Act on 16th June 1854 and then began a series of very lengthy and acrimonious disputes between the two main line companies regarding junction arrangements, branch operations, sharing of London-bound traffic and so on. These sagas have been detailed in many railway histories and so are not amplified here.

After a year of wrangling the Caterham branch opened on 5th August 1856. Bad connections, through ticketing problems, writs and threats of physical actions then ensued. The LBSCR hired rolling stock but the ailing infant Caterham Railway ran at a great loss and could not pay the hire charges in full. Continued antagonistic disputes were halted temporarily on 21st July 1859 when the SER bought the line for less than half its cost. The LBSCR soon retaliated by banning passengers from SER stations from using *its* East Croydon station!

The period 1897-99 saw the doubling of the Caterham branch and the quadrupling of the South Croydon - Stoats Nest section of the main line, along with station improvements.

The SER became known as the South Eastern & Chatham Railway in 1899. This and the LBSCR were incorporated into the Southern Railway in 1923, which in turn became the Southern Region of British Railways upon nationalisation in 1948.

Tattenham Corner branch

The Act for the Chipstead Valley Railway (Purley to Tadworth) was passed on 27th July 1893 and that for the Epsom Downs Extension Railway (to Tattenham Corner) followed in 1894.

A single track, with no intermediate stops, was opened to Kingswood on 1st November 1897 and extended to Tadworth on 1st July 1900. The track doubling was completed in November of that year. Both of the original companies were acquired by the SER.

Completion to Tattenham Corner was achieved on 4th June 1901, which was Derby Day that year. This section received a summer service only, closed in 1914 and reopened in 1928.

Electrification

Both branches benefitted from third-rail traction on 25th March 1928, as did Coulsdon North services. The latter had overhead electrification between 1st April 1925 and 22nd September 1929, giving Purley both forms of traction for a period.

PASSENGER SERVICES

Caterham branch

The first timetable showed four return journeys on weekdays (three on Sundays) but the impecunious company had to reduce this to two daily in 1859. The SER restored services and by 1869 were running 12 weekday trains (four on Sundays).

From 1901 to 1927 the weekday frequency ranged from 19 to 24, except in the latter part of WWI. The advent of electrification in 1928 soon brought a basic 20 minute interval service (30 minutes on Sundays) which continued until 1958, apart from some of the war years and thereafter.

Subsequently there has been an half-hourly service with extras in the peak hours, these working mainly as branch shuttles in 1956-78 as did most trains in the steam era. The majority of trains to London have terminated at Charing Cross although London Bridge has been the more common peak hour destination.

Tattenham Corner branch

Apart from a few summer trains (listed near picture no. 114), all services terminated at Tadworth until 1928.

In the early years there were ten weekday trains, this rising to fourteen by 1910 when there were also four on Sundays. Apart from the war years, the frequency increased steadily to 22 by 1927.

Following electrification the service interval was the same as the Caterham branch, as most down trains divided at Purley. At peak times six coaches went to Caterham and three to Tattenham Corner until 1949 when four-car units were introduced.

Between 1965 and 1970 most branch trains were worked as a shuttle from Purley. Following closure of Coulsdon North in 1983 some additional trains terminated at nearby Smitham.

From May 1986 dividing at Purley ceased (except in peak hours) and the branch received an hourly train to Tattenham Corner and one hourly to Smitham. (A shuttle from Purley operated for a brief period.) These both originated at Victoria, a departure from tradition. Most trains to both branches had for a long time started at Charing Cross, although London Bridge was commonly the starting point in peak hours.

January 1926

LONDON, PURLEY, CATERHAM, TADWORTH AND WALTON-ON-HILL, and TATTENHAM CORNER.—Southern.

LONDON, PURLEY, CATERHAM, TADWORTH AND WALTON-ON-HILL, and TATTENHAM CORNER.—Southern.

1. Purley area

PURLEY

1. The first station opened on 12th July 1841 as "Godstone Road", closed on 1st October 1847 and its passenger shelter was dismantled for use at Bexhill. Here we see one of the few photographs of the second station which came into use on 5th August 1856 as "Caterham Junction". It was renamed "Purley" on 1st October 1888 but there was no direct connection between the branch platform (right) and the main lines. (Pamlin Prints)

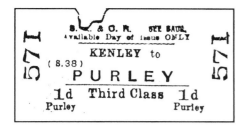

2. The LBSCR rebuilt the station entirely in 1898-99 and provided six platforms, the two on the right for SECR branch trains, the centre two for its own expresses running via its new Quarry Line (which bypassed Redhill) and the other two for its local services. The two extra tracks between South Croydon and Stoats Nest came into use on 5th November 1899. (Lens of Sutton)

3. This is the new entrance provided on the east side of the lines, the main entrance being on the other side. The previous station had received gas lighting in 1867 and a subway in 1874, rather belatedly. (Lens of Sutton)

Other maps and photographs of this station appear in our *East Croydon to Three Bridges* album.

4. The 3.18pm departure for Caterham is on the beginning of the branch on 22nd May 1926, hauled by class H no. A164. Purley South box is on the right and Purley East on the left, ex-LBSCR and SER respectively. The catenary in the background was in use for Coulsdon North trains from 1st April 1925 to 22nd September 1929. (H.C.Casserley)

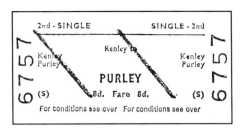

5. The 3.14pm to Tattenham Corner passes Purley East box on the same day in the charge of another H class, no. A518. It will have left London Bridge with the combined trains at 2.40. The footpath in these views was for railway staff only and closed in 1972. East box closed on 18th March 1928, South box taking over its functions. (H.C.Casserley)

6. On the last day of steam operation to Tadworth, H class 0-4-4T no. A520 runs past the electrical sub-station on 24th March 1928. In the foreground is the connection to the engine shed. (H.C.Casserley)

7.   A northward panorama from June 1958 includes all six platforms. By then fast trains used the two tracks on the left. Platforms 3 and 4 had been lengthened to take 12 coach semi-fast trains. A 4EPB stands at platform 6, bound for Tattenham Corner. (Pamlin Prints)

8.   A southward view in May 1955 features the new signal box which came into use on the 8th of that month, superseding North and South boxes. The Tattenham Corner branch passes under the staff footbridge and the Caterham line curves to the left of the sub-station. The box housed a temporary panel from September 1983 until closure on 23rd January 1984. (D.Cullum)

9. Both gas and electric lighting are evident as Q class 0-6-0 no. 30549 works the 8.40am troop train from Caterham through platform 5 on 3rd September 1960. The train was bound for Devynock & Sennybridge, west of Brecon. (J.J.Smith)

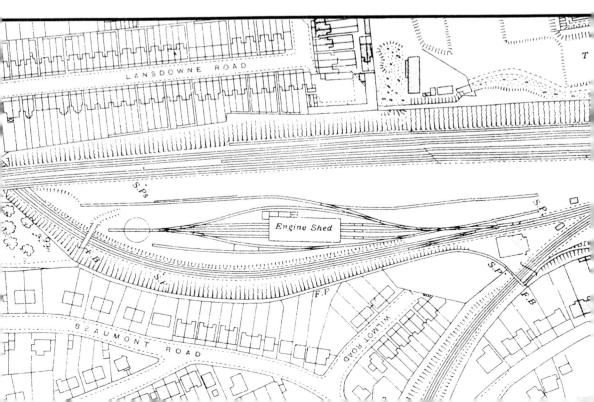

The 1934 map has the London - Brighton main line from right to left, the Tattenham Corner branch passing under it and the Caterham branch running off the bottom of the page.

10. When photographed in 1976 the east side building gave little indication of it being a station. In recent years the adjacent platform 6 has been little used, most trains to both branches using the reversible road at platform 5. (J.Scrace)

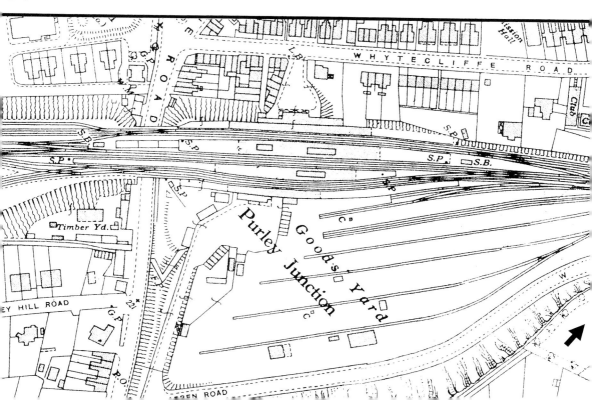

11. A 1989 picture of the main entrance on the west side shows that it retains most of its 1899 features. A subway leads from the booking hall to platforms 2 to 6, the disused no. 1 being once served by the steps on the right. (J.Scrace)

12. Returning from Caterham on 12th March 1988 is the Southern Electric Group's railtour which started at Waterloo and ran via Chessington Goods, Epsom Downs and Norwood Junction to Caterham. It returned via Mitcham Junction, Factory Junction, Angerstein Wharf, Slade Green, Lee Spur, Bromley North, Hayes, Addiscombe, Hampton Court, Staines and Shepperton. There are two 4TC sets behind no. 73138. (J.Scrace)

13.   Purley made an indelible mark in the annals of railway history on 4th March 1989 when the 12.17 from Littlehampton ran into the rear of the 12.50 from Horsham, which had just crossed to the fast line after stopping at the station. Tragically there were five fatalities after five coaches came down the embankment. These had to be recovered by road. (P.Beyer)

14. Although goods facilities were withdrawn on 6th January 1969, part of the yard was retained for aggregate traffic from Cliffe (see picture 20 in our *Branch Line to Allhallows* album). On a misty February day in 1993, no. 60019 is propelling the empty wagons through platform 6, prior to returning them to Cliffe. (V.Mitchell)

15. A few minutes later no. 60019 ran through platform 5 to commence its journey. Comparison with picture no. 8 shows that further alterations were made to allow up branch trains to use platform 4. The footbridge gives staff access to the former engine shed which is used for offices and training purposes. (V.Mitchell)

PURLEY SHED

16. The shed was completed in 1898 and supplied locomotives for SECR suburban and freight services. Purley East box is on the right and we are looking across the Tattenham Corner lines on 22nd May 1926. (H.C.Casserley)

17. This northward view is from the access bridge on the last day of steam, 24th March 1928. The building stored goods wagons for some time and during WWII was the office for the London East District Engineer. The turntable was 50ft in length. (H.C.Casserley)

2. Caterham Branch

KENLEY

18. The new up side platform and booking office is seen just after completion of the branch doubling in 1899. A passing loop had existed here prior to that. (Lens of Sutton)

19. The station was called Coulsdon until December 1856. Kenley was the name of a nearby country house. A similar Alpine style station building can be seen at Betchworth. (R.Packham coll.)

20.   It is apparently nothing new for railway managers to specify clashing architectural styles when extending or otherwise improving stations. The 1899 up side building is on the right. (R.Packham coll.)

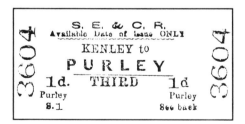

21.   Although apparently built by the independent Caterham Railway the architectural style was similar to that employed on the Redhill - Reading line, although the detailing was very different. (R.Packham coll.)

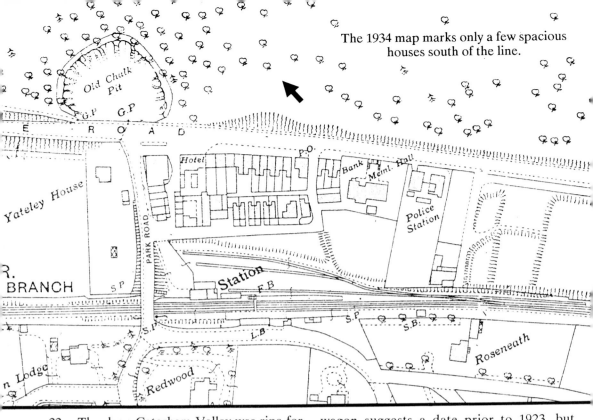

The 1934 map marks only a few spacious houses south of the line.

22. The deep Caterham Valley was ripe for residential development after the railway arrived, the need for doubling reflecting that it took place on a substantial scale. An MR wagon suggests a date prior to 1923, but pre-grouping lettering could still be seen as late as 1930. (Lens of Sutton)

23. The signal box was of typical SER style with weather boards and sash windows. It remained in use until 11th June 1961 but the goods yard closed on 3rd April of that year. (Lens of Sutton)

24. A picture dated 1923 includes much of the scenic downland valley. The parallel line from South Croydon to Oxted is not visible as it is partly in tunnel under the wooded area on the left. The East Surrey Waterworks would have required coal by rail. Its chimney is visible. (H.J.Patterson Rutherford)

25. Steam made a reappearance on passenger stock on the branch on 5th July 1964 when class 2 no. 78038 hauled the LCGB's "Surrey Wanderer". The tour ran from Waterloo via Shepperton, Mitcham, Epsom Downs, Caterham, Tattenham Corner, Kensington Olympia and terminated at Victoria. (S.C.Nash)

26. Unit no. 455823 glides into the down platform on 4th August 1989 working the 13.35 from Charing Cross. The RAF Kenley personnel mostly used Whyteleafe station. (J.Scrace)

SOUTHERN RAILWAY.
Issued subject to the Bye-laws, Regulations & Conditions in the Company's Bills and Notices.
Reedham to
Reedham   Reedham
Tattenham Corner   Tattenham Corner
TATTENHAM CORNER
THIRD CLASS   THIRD CLASS
Fare 1/3   Fare 1/3
NOT TRANSFERABLE.

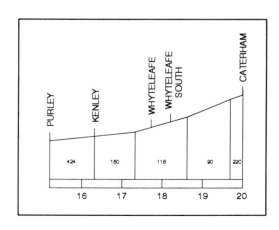

27. Taken on the same day this photograph typifies Kenley - a leafy suburb with a quiet station surrounded by the cars of City workers. (J.Scrace)

WHYTELEAFE

28. The station was opened on 1st January 1900 and is seen nearing completion on 4th September 1899. The signal box in the background was later replaced by a crossing keepers hut and ground frame. A private platform named Halliloo was situated further south but closed when this station opened. (Lens of Sutton)

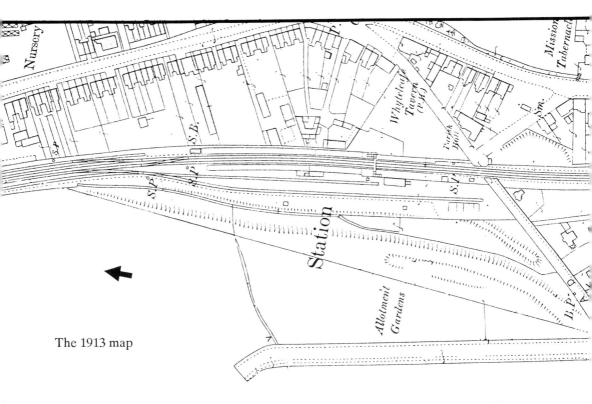

The 1913 map

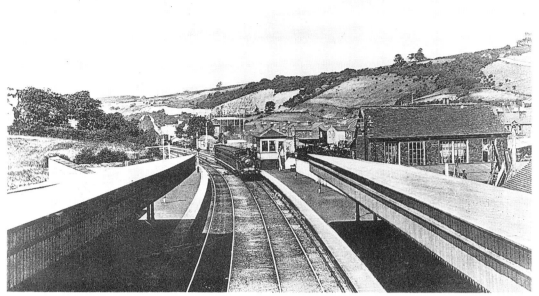

29. The replacement signal box was situated at the opposite end of the down platform, close to the points to the sidings and the crossover. The gasholder in the background was that of Whyteleafe Gasworks which was taken over by the Caterham Gas Co. This was another station to be named after a nearby house. (Lens of Sutton)

30. The building on the left appears to be a signal box; it has no rods or wires and so is presumably an office, probably the station master's. The rods in the foreground may have worked the crossover beyond the gates. (H.C.Casserley coll.)

31.   A view across the valley includes the office, coal wagons in the yard and a train bound for Oxted in the left background. The station was often busy with servicemen for nearby RAF Kenley, which was in use from 1917 to 1988. (R.Packham coll.)

32. A June 1923 picture reveals that the office had been replaced by an SECR wheelbarrow. The post carried stay wires for the signal post opposite. The ringed arm allowed shunt movements to the crossover. The footpath on the right ran to the gate in the centre of the next picture. (H.J.Patterson Rutherford)

33. "Southern Electric" heads the signboard and semi-detached development heads up the hill as the rural delights sought by so many gradually vanish. (Lens of Sutton)

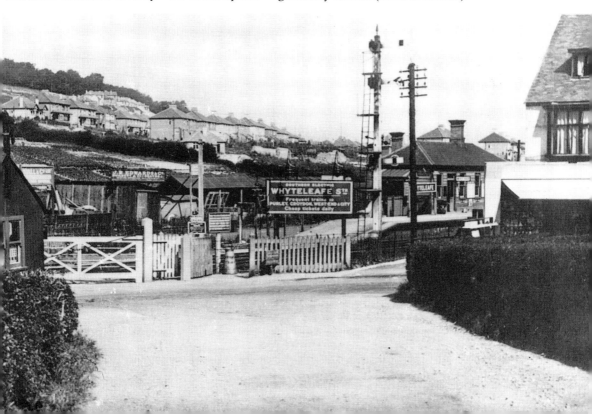

34. The centenary of the Caterham Railway Company was marked with a special train on 6th August 1956. Terrier no. 377S (built as no. 35 *Morden*) was the Brighton Works shunter until withdrawn in 1963 and is seen near the goods yard points. The yard closed on 28th September 1964. (S.C.Nash)

35. Two views from August 1989 reveal that most of the original features remain, although the footbridge had been replaced in 1985. The gates were replaced by controlled barriers on 3rd February 1980, these being worked under CCTV from the box from 18th June 1981. (J.Scrace)

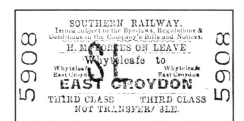

36. Apart from the loss of its chimneys the building was little altered. The signalling had been transformed to colour lights on 25th September 1983. (J.Scrace)

WHYTELEAFE SOUTH

37. The station opened with the line and was known as "Warlingham" until 11th June 1956. This view looks towards Caterham four days earlier when the signs were being changed. (D.Cullum)

38. The signal box dates from 1875 and the nearby footbridge from 1898. The brick structure contains the steps to it. (Lens of Sutton)

39. The signal box was in use until 19th December 1982 when CCTV was installed at the crossing. Note that there was a gate wheel and a mirror which made the signalman's life easier. (Lens of Sutton)

40. The branch freight on 14th December 1963 comprised Q1 class no. 33006, two coal wagons and a brake van. Large amounts of coal had been used in the first three months of that year when the temperature was almost continuously below freezing point. (S.C.Nash)

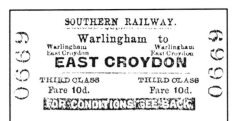

41. Although the station house appears to date from the opening, the offices were built in 1862. Maybe temporary buildings were provided for a trial period. Seen in 1989, the colour light signal came into use on 25th September 1983. (J.Scrace)

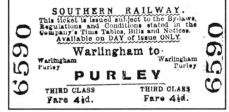

CATERHAM

The 1897 edition features single track and one very short platform. The shed north of the station building survived the alterations.

The 1912 survey (right) emphasises the much greater length of platforms and loops. In view of the universal use of tank engines on passenger trains it is surprising that a turntable was provided.

42. The first station was of the flamboyant style seen at Kenley and was photographed shortly before its demise in 1899. It was situated at the end of a steeply inclined carriage drive. (R.Packham coll.)

43. The offices for the second station were at road level and the passengers had to use a sloping covered passage (right of centre). The drinking fountain is surmounted by a gas lamp. (Lens of Sutton)

S. E. & C. R. (See Back
Available Day of Issue ONLY.
CATERHAM to
PURLEY
10d   First   10d
Purley   Purley

894   894

44. The station received gas lighting in 1873. The new station was provided with engine release crossovers at both platforms. The anticipated traffic in firestone from quarries south of Caterham never materialised. (Lens of Sutton)

45. The station was about one mile from the village but residential and commercial development soon took place around the station. The population rose from 815 in 1861 to 3500 in 1871, doubling again in the following decade. (R.Packham coll.)

46. Long past features include second class compartments (1st and 3rd only from 1923, except on some boat trains), white circles instead of bars on the signal arms and Caterham Electricity Works (near the chimney), once a recipient of rail-borne coal. (D.Cullum coll.)

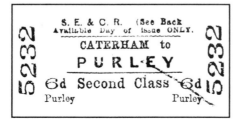

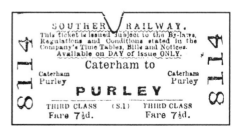

47. The goods shed (left) is believed to have been the engine shed until 1898, when Purley depot came into use. The jib of the 4-ton crane is beyond the coal stack. (D.Cullum coll.)

Copyright
Frith

48. A photograph from the late 1930s is a reminder that buses were bringing many people to the station. The population of the district increased from 12000 in 1921 to 30000 in 1951. The goods yard doubled as the Capitol Cinema car park. (R.Packham coll.)

49. Bunting adorns the passenger platform on 6th August 1956 as the special stands at the goods dock between trips and officials examine the running gear. (R.C.Riley)

50. Track simplification after the end of freight on 28th September 1964 resulted in the sale of much railway land. Unit no. 5652 forms the 09.21 Charing Cross to Caterham on 3rd April 1976. Semaphore signalling ceased and the signal box closed on 25th September 1983. (J.Scrace)

51. On the right is the 10.08 from London Bridge on 11th October 1985, formed of two 4EPB or class 415/4 units. An up train is ready to leave from the other platform. The only berthing siding (right) was still in place in 1993. (C.Wilson)

52. Canopy recladding had been completed by the time this photograph was taken on 3rd July 1989. No. 455836 will depart at 11.39 for Charing Cross. Peak hour departures numbered ten before 09.00. (J.Scrace)

53. The exterior was recorded on the same day. Back in 1930, ten trains left for London before 9.0am and the station issued 146350 tickets and 3895 seasons. Over 15000 tons of goods were handled that year. (J.Scrace)

3. Tattenham Corner Branch

SOUTH OF PURLEY

54. Electric locomotive no. 20002 is hauling the royal train on 4th June 1965, the first year it was not steam worked. Built in 1943, it was fitted with a pantograph for working in the few sidings that were wired overhead. The train is passing the former locomotive shed and is about to pass under the Brighton main line. (J.Scrace)

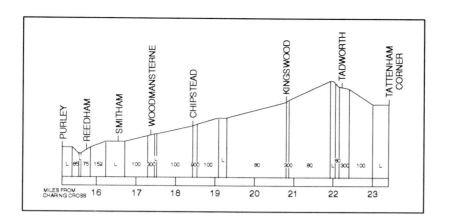

55. Exceptionally heavy snow on 14th January 1987 justified the use of two 4CEP main line units on the branch, the additional power and collector shoes helping in adverse conditions. The apparently disused Brighton main line is in the foreground. (A.Dasi-Sutton)

REEDHAM

56. Reedham Halt was opened on 1st March 1911 but was closed from the first day of 1917 for exactly two years as a wartime economy measure. This northward view is from 1922. (H.J.Patterson Rutherford)

57. The 6.8pm Purley to Tadworth train is seen on 22nd May 1926, hauled by class H 0-4-4T no. A164. The halt was of value to the nearby Reedham Orphanage. (H.C.Casserley)

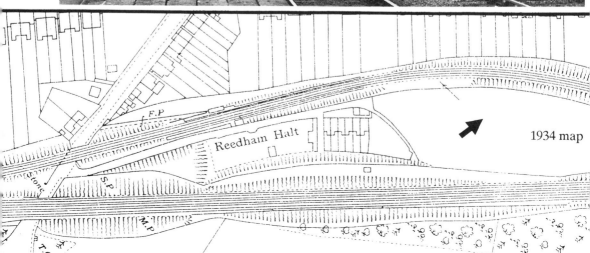

Reedham Halt

1934 map

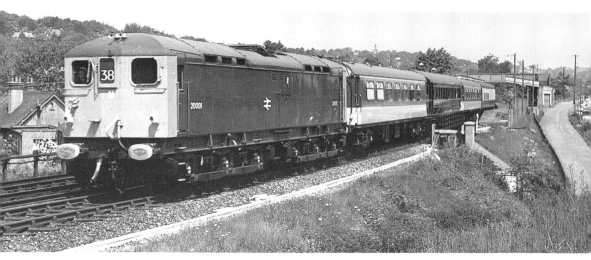

58. Taking the reverse curves through the platforms on 31st May 1968 is the royal train which is headed by no. 20001. This electric locomotive, built in 1941 by the SR and numbered CC1, was one of only three members of the BR class 70. (J.Scrace)

59. The halt became a station on 5th July 1936. This view from the up platform (unusually numbered 2) on 28th April 1982 includes the new coping slabs for use in extending the platforms from six to eight-car length. Smitham was similarly extended at this time. There are 20 mph speed restrictions on the curves under the main line. Some recent time-tables show Reedham (GLC) to distinguish it from Reedham in Norfolk. (C.Evans)

SMITHAM

60. A light engine is on the up line in this 1922 view of the severe 15 chain radius curve which turns the route into the Chipstead Valley. The station came into use on 1st January 1904 and was closed for the same period as Reedham Halt during WWI. (H.J.Patterson Rutherford)

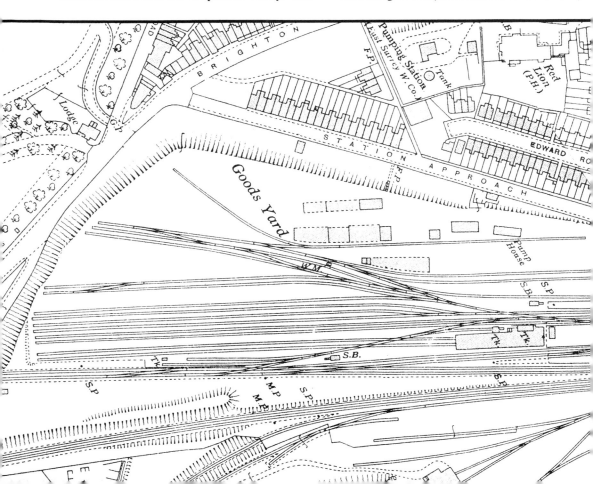

61. Apart from the addition of conductor rails and an upper quadrant signal, little seems to have changed in the fifty years since the opening of the station. Here we look towards Tattenham Corner. (D.Cullum)

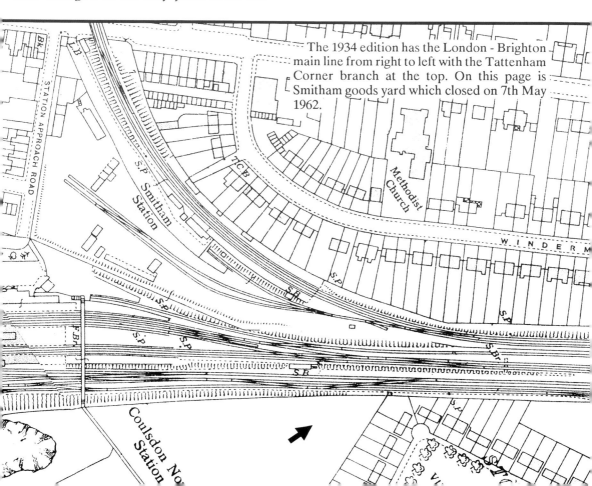

The 1934 edition has the London - Brighton main line from right to left with the Tattenham Corner branch at the top. On this page is Smitham goods yard which closed on 7th May 1962.

62. A northward view from the footbridge over Coulsdon North station on 4th November 1954 shows our route from Purley in the left background. It also reveals the proximity of Coulsdon North to Smitham - its platforms and signal box are on the extreme left. (D.Cullum)

63. Smitham signal box closed on 16th August 1970 when colour light signalling was introduced. In the background is the former LBSCR Coulsdon North box which closed on 23rd January 1984. (J.Scrace)

64. A class 455 unit enters the partially modernised station on 19th September 1989. It was the 12.46 from Victoria, a London terminus that had not been used for branch trains until the closure of Coulsdon North on 1st October 1983. (J.Scrace)

65. The simple profile of an SER station was still evident in 1989 although the original board cladding had been pebble-dashed on this elevation. Some trains have terminated here since 1983, a crossover having been installed north of the station at that time. (J.Scrace)

WOODMANSTERNE

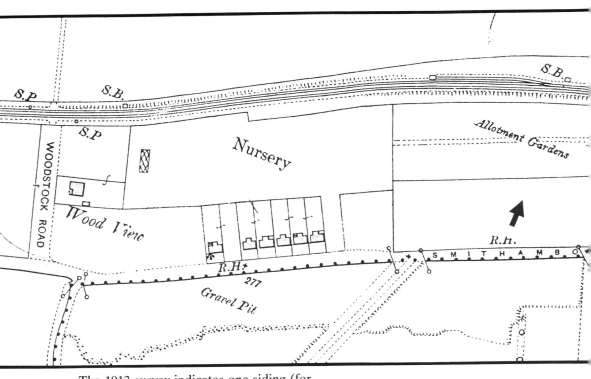

The 1913 survey indicates one siding (for Clock House Farm) but the set in the nursery fence suggests that there had been a gate there on a private siding or that a siding was proposed. The signal box was named Asylum.

The 1933 edition includes a new signal box opened on 13th April 1932 and closed on 12th May 1963.

66. The SR used their much favoured island platform configuration for a new station that opened on 17th July 1932. The concrete foot-bridge gave access to housing developments on both sides of the line. (D.Cullum coll.)

67. No. 33006 was sandwiched between two snowploughs to clear drifts on 15th January 1987. The ploughs are kept at either Norwood Junction or Redhill. The rear plough is near the site of the signal box. (C.Evans)

68. Nature created problems again in 1987 when on October 16th hurricane force winds brought down thousands of trees in south-east England.   De-icer/sandite unit no. 010 was treating the problem of leaves on the line when it was confronted with trees on the line. It was abandoned for two days while the main lines were cleared of thousands of trunks first. (C.Evans)

69. The third natural problem to be illustrated is that of weed growth.   Chipman's weed control train visited the branch from its Horsham base on 26th August 1993.   In the background is the new steel footbridge, a typical product of the mid 1980s. No. 20500 is leading with no. 20503 at the rear, both being on hire from Hunslet Barclay. (C.Evans)

CHIPSTEAD

70. Initially this was the only intermediate station on the branch to Kingswood and opened on 1st November 1897. It was provided with a passing loop until the track was doubled in 1900. (Lens of Sutton)

The 1933 map indicates the cutting necessary to accommodate the single siding.

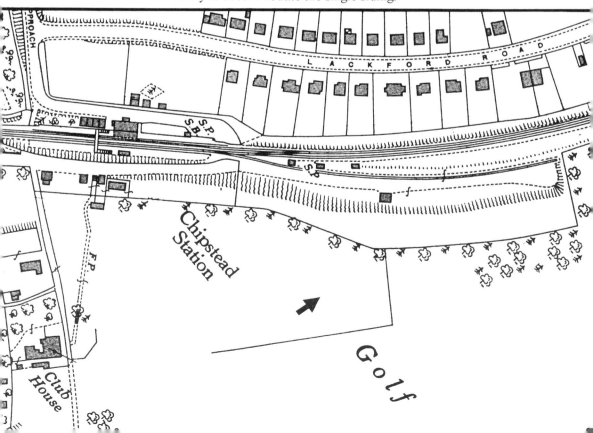

71. The building was far superior to the later SECR structure at Smitham. Its situation on the side of Chipstead Valley is clear in this eastward view. (R.Packham coll.)

72. A down train is on the 1 in 100 up gradient on 2nd August 1926, the locomotive being H class 0-4-4T no. A261. It was working the 10.37am bank holiday special from Purley to Tattenham Corner. (H.C.Casserley)

73. The grass round the gates shows that they were little used. It seems that their original purpose had been to give access to the goods yard. They carried no lamps. (D.Cullum coll.)

←

74. A train loaded with racegoers passes through on 6th June 1953 while class K 2-6-0 no. 32353 waits in the yard on royal train standby duty. The wider second coach was one of those added to the 3SUB sets in 1949. (Pamlin Prints)

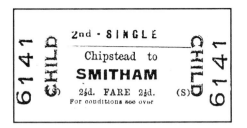

2nd · SINGLE

Chipstead to
SMITHAM

2½d. FARE 2½d. (S)

For conditions see over

CHILD 6141   CHILD 6141

75. Working the 10.07 from Tattenham Corner to Purley on 26th February 1983 is one of the 2EPB sets introduced to the branch in 1974. The barrow crossing in the background seems to have been added after the level crossing was lost. (A.Dasi-Sutton)

76. Approaching Chipstead on 1st June 1983 is no. 73142 *Broadlands*, the first choice for royal train working for many years. With dual power, the class 73 has "belt and braces", of value on such special occasions. (J.S.Petley)

77. A 1989 northward panorama conveys the rural ambience that still existed. Note the footbridge extension, not shown on the 1933 map. The goods facilities had been withdrawn on 7th May 1962. (J.Scrace)

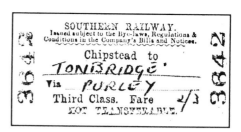

SOUTHERN RAILWAY.
Issued subject to the Bye-laws, Regulations & Conditions in the Company's Bills and Notices.

Chipstead to
TONBRIDGE
Via PURLEY
Third Class. Fare 2/3
NOT TRANSFERABLE.

78. The up side building was still complete when recorded in July 1992, although not in use. A plastic cabin was provided for early morning ticket issue, although this seems to have been little used. (F.Hornby)

79. South of Chipstead the line crosses Chipstead Bottom and the B2032 on this unusual viaduct. The arch to the right of the steel span has been bricked in and the whole structure is subject to a 20mph speed limit. Class K 2-6-0 no. 32340 is on its way from Norwood Shed to Tattenham Corner on 14th December 1958 to fetch 19 vans stored there. They would be taken to New Cross Gate to work the pre-Christmas parcel traffic. (J.J.Smith)

KINGSWOOD

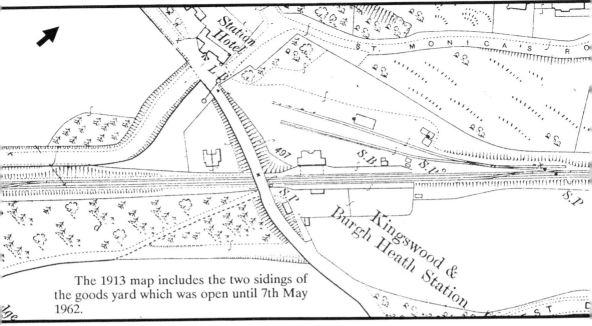

The 1913 map includes the two sidings of the goods yard which was open until 7th May 1962.

80. The impressively styled station had been the terminus of the branch from 1st November 1897 until 1st July 1900. The signal post devoid of an arm may have been for starting up trains from the down platform during the terminal period. (Lens of Sutton)

81. An up train is approaching as the photographer records the novel platform canopy which doubled as an extension to the first floor refreshment room, teas being served on it until the 1920s. The signal box was in use until 2nd December 1962. (Lens of Sutton)

82. Looking down the 1 in 80 gradient towards Chipstead we are unable to see Chipstead Intermediate signal box or the catch point on the down line, but we can observe track maintenance in progress. (Lens of Sutton)

83. This was the local station for Mr. Cosmo Bonsor who was one of the promoters of the line, a director of the SER and its chairman from 1898. This would account for its elegant styling. The drive from his house (Kingswood Warren) passed under the road and parallel to the tracks (see map). The arch served as a shelter for his horse drawn transport during the day. (Lens of Sutton)

84. A 1951 photograph includes the W.H.Smith stall and the concrete footbridge provided prior to electrification. Behind this is the sub-station which housed rotary convertors until 1955 when they were replaced by mercury arc rectifiers. (D.Cullum coll.)

2nd SINGLE SINGLE 2nd

Kingswood & Burgh Heath to

Kingswood
Purley or Reedham

Kingswood
Purley or Reedham

PURLEY or REEDHAM
(S) 1/- FARE 1/- (S)
For conditions see over For conditions see over

0422

0422

85. The royal train stock is returning from Tattenham Corner on 29th May 1963, the locomotive being no. 34088 *213 Squadron* seen on the cover on the outward journey. H. M. The Queen usually returned by road. The signal box closed on 2nd December 1962. (Lens of Sutton)

86. The station served an area of well spaced large residences and when pictured in 1982 it retained much of its original dignity. However the down platform shelter had been replaced by an austere modern type. (F.Hornby)

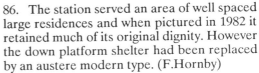

SOUTHERN RAILWAY.
This Ticket is issued subject to the By-laws
Regulations & Conditions stated in the
Company's Time Tables Bills & Notices
Available on DAY of issue ONLY.
Tadworth & Walton-on-Hill to
Tadworth   Tadworth
East Croydon   East Croydon
EAST   CROYDON
THIRD CLASS   THIRD CLASS
Fare 1/4   Fare 1/4

7852   7852

87. A 1989 record shows the building to be partly occupied by an estate agent. The booking office and hall were still retained for use on weekday mornings. The goods yard had closed on 7th May 1962. (J.Scrace)

88. A photograph dated 1898 includes a steam driven excavator on the centre road. The locomotive is a Manning Wardle 0-6-0ST, similar to *Sidlesham* that appears in our *Branch Line to Selsey*. (Mrs. G.J.Smith coll.)

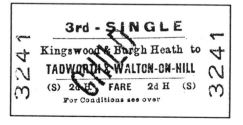

89. After climbing at 1 in 80 from Kingswood, the branch reaches its summit on an 18-chain curve under Tadworth Street bridge. Here it turns from a westerly to a northerly direction. (D.Cullum coll.)

PURLEY AND TADWORTH and WALTON-ON-HILL.—South Eastern and Chatham.

January 1901

TADWORTH

90. The station was opened on 1st July 1900 in a thinly populated district with a view to attracting residential development. This it did successfully. Nearby Walton-on-the-Hill generated additional traffic. (D.Cullum coll.)

91. 0-6-0 no. 41 was rebuilt to class 01 in 1908 and is seen in that form at the down platform with a Birdcage coach attached. This typical SECR formation will have just passed through the 310 yd Kingswood Tunnel and the 37 yd Hoppity Tunnel. Tunnel Intermediate box was situated between the two tunnels and, like Chipstead Intermediate, was only in use on race days. (Lens of Sutton)

92. This northward view features the covered way to the up platform and also the goods yard. The line drops at 1 in 100 in the distance towards Tattenham Corner. (D.Cullum coll.)

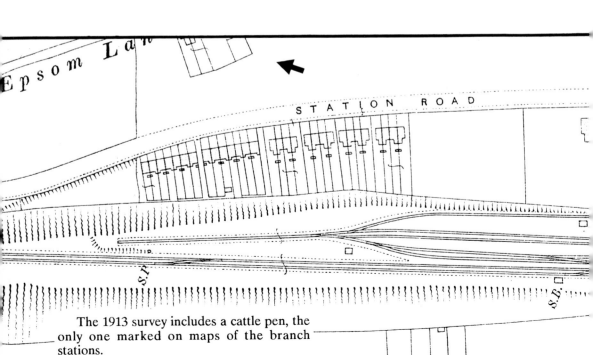

The 1913 survey includes a cattle pen, the only one marked on maps of the branch stations.

93. A light engine stands in the gloom by the water tank and the high level station offices. Mock Tudor facades adorn the dwellings above the new shops. (D.Cullum coll.)

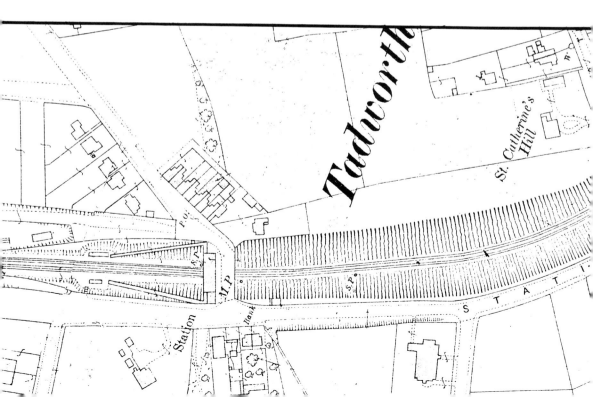

94. The 4.2pm Tadworth to Purley service on 16th April 1927 was worked by class H 0-4-4T no. A193. This was the last complete year that Tadworth would be the terminating point for most branch trains. (H.C.Casserley)

95. The goods yard closed on 7th May 1962 and on 5th July 1964 the LCGB railtour passed its site after visiting Tattenham Corner behind class M7 no. 30053. This locomotive was to be found working on the Swanage Railway in the 1990s after a long period in North America. (S.C.Nash)

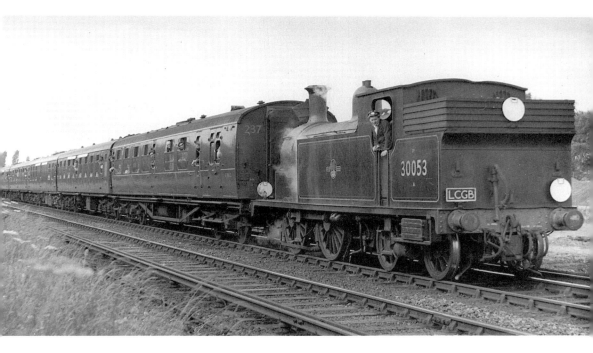

96. A 1988 picture reveals that all the station offices were in commercial use, platform access being at the side. The small canopy was removed later. (A.N.Davenport)

97. By the time the platforms were recorded in 1992 they had become greatly overshadowed by uncontrolled tree growth, which also added to the problems of leaves on the lines. A small ticket office was provided on the up platform. This office had been renovated and improved in 1988. (J.Scrace)

98. Class 455 units were introduced to the branch in May 1986 and were subsequently fitted with radios prior to DOO (driver only operation). "Test Car Iris" is passing through while testing the strength of the radio signals for the numerous transmitter masts that had been erected. The gap in the conductor rails marks the site of the staff crossing. (P.Beyer)

99. The 13.46 from Victoria on 16th September 1992 was worked by a class 456 two-car set. These were introduced to the route in October 1991. Tickets were available from a travelling conductor (south of Purley) or a machine (right). As at other stations this side of Smitham, the platforms could only accommodate six cars. (J.Scrace)

TATTENHAM CORNER

100. The station opened on 4th June 1901 and was intended for recreational traffic - Epsom Races and visitors to Epsom Downs. Six passenger platforms were provided together with berthing for 24 trains. (Lens of Sutton)

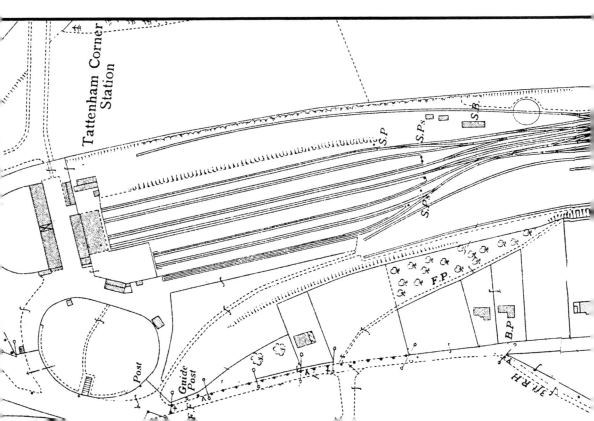

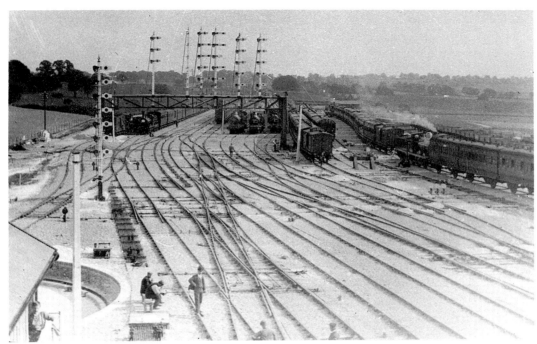

101. The turntable pit (lower left) seems clean, suggesting that this photograph was taken soon after the opening. Note that four-wheeled coaches were still in use. (Lens of Sutton)

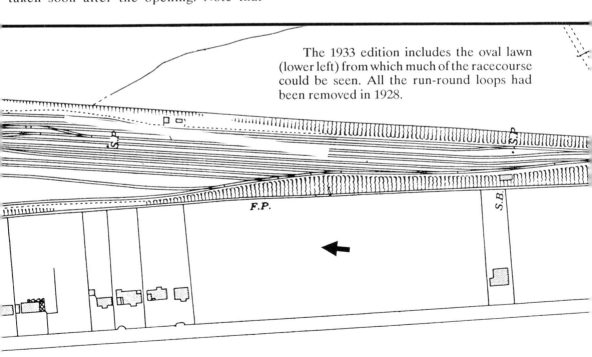

The 1933 edition includes the oval lawn (lower left) from which much of the racecourse could be seen. All the run-round loops had been removed in 1928.

F.P.

S.B.

102.   The two previous pictures were taken from the gantry on the left of this view. The signal arms are numbered 1 to 5 from top to bottom, each post applying to a different arrival road. In the early years, no advance plans were made, an inspector being left to make impromptu arrangements on race days. (Lens of Sutton)

103.   The commodious station was ideal for handling large numbers of troops in World War I. Antiquated close coupled stock is in the background. (R.Packham coll.)

July 1906

PURLEY, KINGSWOOD, and TATTENHAM CORNER.—South Eastern and Chatham.

s Saturdays only. • Chipstead and Banstead Downs. † Kingswood and Burgh Heath. ‡ Tadworth and Walton-on-Hill. § Epsom Downs.

104.   Military camps were established on
Epsom Downs and the station was closed to
the public in September 1914. There is railway
activity in the background. (R.Packham coll.)

105. During WWI the government established the Railway Operating Department which obtained many 2-8-0s to help with military transport in Europe. Part of this fleet was photographed on 14th February 1920 awaiting sale, over 100 having been stored here in the previous year. Also included are some of the military buildings. In 1973, 4 COR units were stored here awaiting scrapping. (H.C.Casserley)

106. "B" Box is shown on the right of the map. It controlled access to the sidings and was a block post until 18th February 1966. In latter years it had 50 levers. (Lens of Sutton)

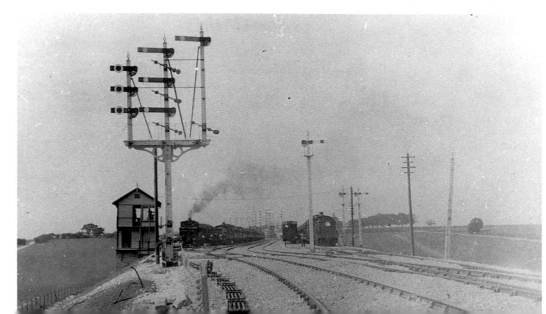

107. SECR no. 812 was an N class 2-6-0 built at Ashford in 1920. The van was required for the guard only - the Pullman cars had no accommodation for him. Horse boxes are in the background - at least two bear the initials GW. (Lens of Suton)

BUFF
TICKETS.
CARS
↓
K
L
M
N
O
P
R
S

BLUE
TICKETS.
CARS
↓
A
B
C
D
E
F
G
H

1922-24 period. On Derby Day in 1923 about 40,000 passengers departed from this station. (Lens of Sutton)

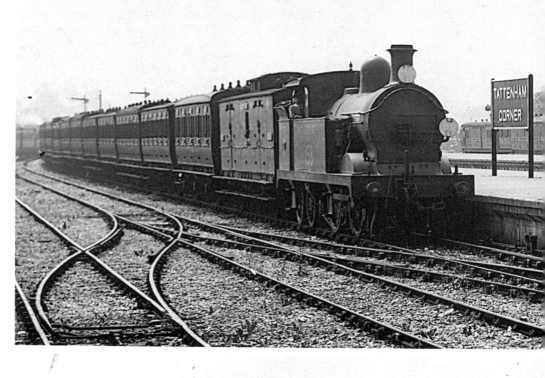

109. On bank holidays many Londoners were attracted to the breezy heights of Epsom Downs where various fairground entertainments were on offer. This is the scene on the penultimate steam worked August bank holiday, 2nd August 1926. Class H 0-4-4T no. A158 is ready to come off its train after arrival. (H.C.Casserley)

110. This is the signalman's view shortly after the completion of electrification in 1928. Alterations included removal of the centre engine release roads and the associated points seen in the previous picture. (National Railway Museum)

111. There were no platform canopies but this extensive shelter was provided between the platform ends and the offices, and was photographed in 1947. The small signal box was designated "C" and seems to have controlled the crossovers until 1928. (H.C.Casserley coll.)

DERBY DAY ROYAL TRAINS
FOR QUEEN ELIZABETH II
Compiled by K.C.Brodrick

1953	"Schools" class 30915 *Brighton*	1974	Class 31 diesel loco 31295
1954	"Schools" class 30936 *Cranleigh*	1975	Class 31 diesel loco 31258
1955	"Schools" class 30933 *King's Canterbury*	1976	Class 31 diesel loco 31257
1956	No train due to strike	1977	Class 31 diesel loco 31414
1957	"Schools" class 30939 *Leatherhead*	1978	Class 73 electro-diesel loco 73123
1958	"Schools" class 30908 *Westminster*	1979	Class 73 electro-diesel loco 73142 *Broadlands*
1959	"Schools" class 30938 *St Olave's*	1980	Class 73 electro-diesel loco 73142 *Broadlands*
1960	"Schools" class 30925 *Cheltenham*	1981	Class 73 electro-diesel loco 73142 *Broadlands*
1961	"Schools" class 30926 *Repton*	1982	Class 73 electro-diesel loco 73142 *Broadlands*
1962	"Schools" class 30926 *Repton*	1983	Class 73 electro-diesel loco 73142 *Broadlands*
1963	"Battle of Britain" class 34088 *213 Squadron*	1984	Class 73 electro-diesel loco 73142 *Broadlands*
1964	"Battle of Britain" class 34052 *Lord Dowding*	1985	Class 73 electro-diesel loco 73142 *Broadlands*
1965	Electric loco 20002	1986	Class 73 electro-diesel loco 73142 *Broadlands*
1966	Electric loco 20003	1987	Class 73 electro-diesel loco 73142 *Broadlands*
1967	Electric loco 20003	1988	Class 73 electro-diesel loco 73201 *Broadlands*
1968	Electric loco 20001	1989	Class 73 electro-diesel loco 73201 *Broadlands*
1969	Class 31 diesel loco 5518 (later 31101)	1990	Class 73 electro-diesel loco 73201 *Broadlands*
1970	Class 31 diesel loco 5659 (later 31232)	1991	Class 73 electro-diesel loco 73201 *Broadlands*
1971	Class 31 diesel loco 5659 (later 31232)	1992	Class 73 electro-diesel loco 73202 *Royal Observer Corps*
1972	Class 31 diesel loco 5688 (later 31260)		
1973	Class 31 diesel loco 5690 (later 31262)	1993	Class 73 electro-diesel loco 73201 *Broadlands*

112. This 1950 picture shows that watering facilities were retained for race and goods trains. The flange at the top of the column was inclined so that the bearing wheel ran to the lowest part (as shown) to prevent the arm swinging onto a passing train. Note the ex-SECR perforated concrete signal posts. (A.N.Davenport)

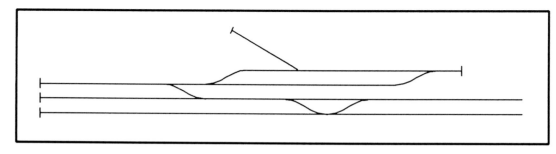

Track layout since 1971. All but the shortest
siding are electrified.

113. Five of the platform roads had conductor rails but none of the sidings did. Berthing of electric stock therefore had to be undertaken by ex-LBSCR engines as only these were fitted with air pumps. Here a K class 2-6-0 has been coupled to 2EPB set no. 5753. (D.Cullum coll.)

114. The 54ft turntable was pictured on 10th May 1957 as class 4 2-6-4T no. 42082 propelled the weed killing train along the little used siding behind the signal box. (A.N.Davenport)

The figures below show the number of trains timetabled for the month of July in the years listed. An additional train ran on Saturday afternoons. No trains were operated in winter months.

	Weekdays	Sundays
1904	5	4
1906	3	2
1908	3	-
1910	7	-
1912	6	-
1914	6	-

No regular service operated between 1914 and 1928.

115. On the 15th May 1958 the royal train was composed of Pullman cars. After their demise, designated royal train coaches were used. The locomotive is "Schools" class 4-4-0 no. 30908 *Westminster*. (P.Hay)

N O T I C E
OF
R O Y A L   T R A I N
WEDNESDAY, 25th and FRIDAY, 27th MAY, 1966

Distance from Victoria			arr.	dep.
m.	c.			
—	—	VICTORIA	..	12 10
		(*Platform* 15, *South Section*)	(Through Line)	
2	57	Clapham Junction		12 15½
4	69	Balham Junction		12 18 (Through Line)
10	04	Windmill Bridge Junction ..		12 23½ (Through Line)
10	45	East Croydon		12 24½
11	37	South Croydon		12 25½
13	46	Purley		12 28½
15	00	Smitham		12 32
16	74	Chipstead		12 36
19	25	Kingswood	..	..
20	51	Tadworth	..	..
21	70	TATTENHAM CORNER .. (*Platform* 5)	12 45	..

116. The exterior continued to display its SER ancestry when recorded in 1978. Hipped roofs and timber cladding could be found throughout that system. An 11KV cable links the power supply here to that at Epsom Downs station. (F.Hornby)

WEDNESDAY, 25th AND FRIDAY, 27th MAY—*continued*

Formation of 12 10 Victoria to Tattenham Corner

ELECTRIC LOCOMOTIVE No. 20003

Gangways to be Connected
{
Pullman Car " No. 208 " (Brake leading)—For Railway Officers.
Eastern Region Saloon No. 396 (Saloon trailing)—For H.M. The Queen.
Pullman Car " Aquila " (Kitchen trailing)—For Royal Household.
Pullman Car " Isle of Thanet " (Brake trailing)—For Servants.
}

EMPTY TRAINS:—

	arr.	dep.
Stewarts Lane	A	11†15
Victoria (*Platform 15—South Section*) ..	11†20	..

Form 12 10 to Tattenham Corner

A—The locomotive to work the 12 10 " Royal " Victoria to Tattenham Corner will also work the 11 15 empty from Stewarts Lane.

Inspector J. Bull will travel with the empty train from Stewarts Lane to Victoria.

Formation leaving Stewarts Lane:—

Electric Locomotive No. 20003

Gangways to be Connected
{
Pullman Car " Isle of Thanet " (Brake leading).
Pullman Car " Aquila " (Kitchen leading).
Eastern Region Saloon No. 396 (Saloon leading).
Pullman Car " No. 208 " (Brake trailing).
}

Formed of 12 10 Victoria	Wednesday 25th May		Friday 27th May	
	arr.	dep.	arr.	dep.
Tattenham Corner	..	13†30	..	13†52
Chipstead	13 40		14 02	
Smitham	13 44		14 07	
Purley	13 48		14 12F	14 18
East Croydon	13 54	13 55	14¶25	14 32
				(Local Line)
Windmill Bridge Junction	13 56		14 33	
	(Through Line)		(Local Line)	
Selhurst	13 58		14 36	
	(Local Line)		(Local Line)	
Streatham Common	14 06		14 43	
Streatham	14 08½		14 45½	
Tulse Hill	14 12		14 49	
Herne Hill	14 19		14 54	
Brixton	14 21		14 55½	
Stewarts Lane	14†30	..	15†05	..

608

Passengers mu[st]
not cross the li[ne]

Danger

Do not touch
the live rail

117. The first box was designated "A" and originally had an amazing 205 levers. This had been reduced to 125 prior to its destruction by fire on 15th July 1924. This box dates from 6th April 1925 and was closed on 25th September 1983 when control of the area from Victoria Panel commenced. The colour light signals came into use on 29th November 1970. This 2EPB was recorded on 27th May 1985. (A.N.Davenport)

118. Drifts to platform height on 15th January 1987 confirmed this location as not being ideal for stock berthing. It was its extensive platforms which gave rise to this practice from the advent of electrification. Eight 3 SUB units were kept here overnight in 1946. In 1993 there were two 455s and two 456s. (P.Beyer)

BRITISH RAILWAYS (S)
This ticket is issued subject to the bye-laws, Regulations and Conditions contained in the Publications and Notices of and applicable to the Railway Executive.
Kingswood & Burgh Heath to
Kingswood Kingswood
Tattenham Corner Tattenham Corner
TATTENHAM CORNER
THIRD CLASS   THIRD CLASS
Fare 5 1.   Fare 8d.
NOT TRANSFERABLE.

0324   0324

119. This 1988 photograph shows the numbering of the three platforms that had been in use since 29th November 1970. Originally the numbering was 1 to 6 from right to left but this was reversed on 6th April 1924. (A.N.Davenport)

120. The impressive shelter was recorded in November 1989, along with the entrance to the booking hall and traincrew room. All were still in use in 1993 when the station provided a good place to leave the car and "let the train take the strain". (V.Mitchell)

Other photographs of both branches can be seen in Peter Hay's
Steaming through Surrey
(Middleton Press).

MP Middleton Press

Easebourne Lane, Midhurst. West Sussex. GU29 9AZ   Tel: (0730) 813169 Fax: (0730) 812601
. . . . . *Write or telephone for our latest list* . . . . .

BRANCH LINES

Branch Line to Allhallows
Branch Lines to Alton
Branch Lines tround Ascot
Branch Lines to East Grinstead
Branch Lines tround Effingham Jn
Branch Lines to Exmouth
Branch Line to Fairford
Branch Lines around Gosport
Branch Line to Hawkhurst
Branch Line to Hayling
Branch Lines to Horsham
Branch Lines around Huntingdon
Branch Lines to Ilfracombe
Branch Lines to Longmoor
Branch Line to Lyme Regis
Branch Line to Lynton
Branch Lines around March
Branch Lines around Midhurst
Branch Line to Minehead
Branch Lines to Newport
Branch Lines around Portmadoc (1923-46)
Branch Lines to Seaton & Sidmouth
Branch Line to Selsey
Branch Lines around Sheerness
Branch Line to Shrewsbury
Branch Line to Southwold
Branch Line to Swanage
Branch Line to Tenterden
Branch Lines to Tunbridge Wells
Branch Lines tround Weymouth
Branch Lines around Wimborne

LONDON SUBURBAN RAILWAYS

Charing Cross to Dartford
Crystal Palace and Catford Loop
Holborn Viaduct to Lewisham
Kingston and Hounslow Loops
Lewisham to Dartford
London Bridge to Addiscombe
Mitcham Junction Lines
West Croydon to Epsom

STEAMING THROUGH

Steaming through East Hants
Steaming through the Isle of Wight
Steaming through Surrey
Steaming through West Hants
Steaming through West Sussex

SOUTH COAST RAILWAYS

Ashford to Dover
Bournemouth to Weymouth
Brighton to Eastbourne
Brighton to Worthing
Chichester to Portsmouth
Dover to Ramsgate
Eastbourne to Hastings
Hastings to Ashford
Southampton to Bournemouth

SOUTHERN MAIN LINES

Basingstoke to Salisbury
Bromley South to Rochester
Charing Cross to Orpington
Crawley to Littlehampton
East Croydon to Three Bridges
Epsom to Horsham
Exeter to Barnstaple
Faversham to Dover
Haywards Heath to Seaford
London Bridge to East Croydon
Orpington to Tonbridge
Salisbury to Yeovil
Sittingbourne to Ramsgate
Three Bridges to Brighton
Tonbridge to Hastings
Victoria to Bromley South
Victoria to East Croydon
Waterloo to Windsor
Waterloo to Woking
Woking to Southampton
Yeovil to Exeter

COUNTRY RAILWAY ROUTES

Andover to Southampton
Bath To Evercreech Junction
Bournemouth to Evercreech Jn
Burnham to Evercreech Junction
East Kent Light Railway
Fareham to Salisbury
Guildford to Redhill
Reading to Guildford
Redhill to Ashford
Strood to Paddock Wood
Woking to Alton
Yeovil to Dorchester

TRAMWAY CLASSICS

Brighton's Tramways
Camberwell & W. Norwood Tramwa
Dover's Tramways
Greenwich & Dartford Tramways
Hastings Tramways
Thanet's Tramways

BUS BOOKS

Eastbourne Bus Story
Tillingbourne Bus Story

OTHER RAILWAY BOOKS

Garraway Father & Son
Industrial Railways of the South Eas
London Chatham & Dover Railway
South Eastern Railway
War on the Line
West Sussex Railways in the 1980s

MILITARY BOOKS

Battle Over Portsmouth
Battle Over Sussex 1940
Military Defence of West Sussex

WATERWAY ALBUMS

Hampshire Waterways
Kent and East Sussex Waterways
West Sussex Waterways

COUNTRY BOOKS

Betwixt Petersfield and Midhurst
Brickmaking in Sussex
East Grinstead Then and Now
Leigh Park
Walking Ashdown Forest